Glass Ramps/Glass Wall
Deviations from the Normative

Bernard Tschumi and Hugh Dutton

Project by
Bernard Tschumi
Gruzen Samton
Ove Arup and Partners

Architectural Association

Glass Ramps/Glass Wall

Glass Ramps / Glass Wall
Deviations from the Normative

Authors: Bernard Tschumi, Hugh Dutton, Jesse Reiser

AA Publications are initiated by the Chairman of the Architectural Association, Mohsen Mostafavi.

Glass Ramps/Glass Wall has been edited by Pamela Johnston, designed by Nicola Bailey,
and produced through the AA Print Studio with Clare Barrett and Mark Rappolt (editorial assistants)
and Marilyn Sparrow (art assistant).

ISBN 1 902902 00 9
Printed in Italy by Grafiche Milani

A catalogue of AA Publications is available from:
AA Publications
Architectural Association
36 Bedford Square
London WC1B 3ES
T. 020 7887 4021
F. 020 7414 0782
E. publications@aaschool.ac.uk
www.aaschool.ac.uk/publications

Deviations from the Normative

Project Credits

This book documents one specific part of a complex building. By emphasizing the particular glass and steel technology used in Lerner Hall, it tries to show that architecture need not be unitary or homogeneous, but that special constructive devices can be applied to certain parts of a building and deviate from other, more conventional ones, so that the building becomes a hybrid between the old and the new, the traditional and the inventive. A very large team was involved with the making of Lerner Hall. As with the making of a film, we would like to start this book with the credits.

Building	Alfred Lerner Hall
Location	115th Street + Broadway, Columbia University, New York City
Design	1994 – 1995
Construction	Fall 1996 – Summer 1999
Architects	Bernard Tschumi / Gruzen Samton
Principals in charge	Bernard Tschumi, Peter Samton
Project team	Bernard Tschumi Architects
	Bernard Tschumi, Tom Kowalski, Megan Miller, Kim Starr, Mark Haukos, Ruth Berktold, Richard Veith, Galia Solomonoff, Yannis Aesopos, Tony Manzo, Peter Cornell, Jordan Parnass, Stacy Norman
	Gruzen Samton Architects
	Peter Samton, Tim Schmiderer, David Terenzio, Ken Hutchinson, Jerzy Lesniak, Scott Broaddus, Liane Williams-Liu, Geoff Doban, Nick Lombardo, John Mulling, Nicholas Hedin, Cameron Lory, Jo Goldberger

Client	Columbia University
Engineers	Special structures (suspended ramps and glass walls) Ove Arup and Partners, New York Hugh Dutton Associates, Paris
	Steel and concrete structures Severud Associates, New York
	Building services (MEP) Ove Arup and Partners, New York
	Fire engineers Arup Fire, New York
Consultants	Lighting Ove Arup and Partners, New York
	Acoustical (Theatre Consultant) David Harvey Associates, New York Peter George Associates, New York
Profit centre designers	Dining Services Thomas Ricca Associates, Englewood, Colorado
	Bookstore Antunovich Associates, Chicago
	Banking Centre Gensler, San Francisco
Construction manager	Barney Skanska Construction, New York
Contractors (glass ramps/ glass wall)	Eiffel Construction Métallique, France Precision, New York Saint-Gobain, France Sun Glass, Italy
Photographs	Peter Mauss/ESTO, Judith Turner, David Ternzio, Hugh Dutton, Bernard Tschumi

The late architectural critic Robin Evans once famously commented that architects don't make buildings – they make drawings and models of buildings. While these instruments place the architect at some remove from physical construction, they nevertheless amplify his effectiveness within a wider field than labour alone and thus initiate a complex mechanics of directives, conditioned by legal limits and promising social contracts. Ultimately, however, the full range of material arrangements, political and social desires, and affects is determined by the organization of matter in space.

Introduction
Jesse Reiser

Bernard Tschumi, Hugh Dutton, Gruzen Samton, Ove Arup and Partners and the administration and Trustees of Columbia University 'mobilized a mixture of human and non-human agents in a "productive" controversy' that led to a building. At stake was the legitimacy of a nineteenth-century master plan and the desire for a truly innovative campus architecture. What arose is not a testament to realism or the reality of compromises in real-life building. Nor is it about an abstract contest between realism and idealism (they are two poles of the same argument); it is, rather, a turbulent mixture conditioned by advances and retreats. The effective dimension of this architecture de-individualizes the architect's signature and, in the same measure, thrusts the impersonal individuation of the built field to the fore. Indeed, it is only through this field of material relations, and the flows animating them, that the active capacity of this architecture becomes possible.

On first inspection the Columbia campus enforces what would appear to be a solid logic, i.e. solid buildings on a solid base, which would imply clear divisions between what is campus and what is not, as well as between the various disciplines that each university building houses. But this could not be further from the truth; in reality, the campus plinth, like the buildings that sit on it, is a sheathed skeleton. Moreover, the campus and building skeletons are co-extensive, as are the materials that clad them. Lerner Hall is a hiatus in these linked continua: it is not so much an invasion of the campus structure by a foreign element as a singular irruption between systems of structure and cladding. A new relationship is revealed by the division of the building into opaque Broadway and campus wings that flank a transparently clad middle. Within this middle zone, the taut treatment of the ramp and curtain wall layers registers the dilation and contraction of structural and social flows. In effect, Tschumi elaborates the underlying structural skeleton as a series of ramped bridges that bloom into the free space defined by the building volume. This object of contained flow might be seen to represent an ideal of what the campus could become, should its organization permeate the campus proper. The building's critical and even Utopian status has to do with the fact that it frames this condition as a tableau vivant. This representational moment is, in actuality, the after-effect of a coherent systemic move to establish the building's role, not as an object, but as a flow-space linking the campus and its context.

It is perhaps ironic and yet fitting, given the context of the building in the McKim master plan, that a nineteenth-century set-piece battle of engineering versus architecture is now waged once again. The major elements of Lerner Hall are directly analogous to those of bridges; and like steel bridge design from the nineteenth century into the twentieth, it faced similar resistance from conservative ideologies. In its simplest form, a bridge consists of a span connected at either end by abutments, the elements which transmit the loads of the span into the earth. A typical nineteenth-century compromise between engineering logic and the conservative ideals of symbolic fortitude and ceremony was to clad the steel structure of the abutments with a stone facing while leaving the spanning element a visible and pure resolution of material and forces. Similarly, the central zone of Lerner Hall develops in space as a spectacular multi-tiered bridge whose masonry-clad wings form opaque abutments to Broadway and the campus. This uneasy coupling of the conventional with the innovative is readily seized upon by conservative critics, whose interpretations are generally semiotic. It does not, however, weaken or dilute the genuine novelty of the middle zone, whose essential newness is performative, being only secondarily representational. (In a similar way, the operationality of liquid-crystal display does not depend upon the style of its frame.)

Lerner Hall might best be understood, not as a deviation from the norm, but as a complex ecology. Any building can be understood as the result of negotiations among a constellation of political entities, codes, desires, programmes and technical assemblies. But not every building is an ecology – although systematicity is a precondition, even buildings that are inherently systemic are not necessarily ecological. For example, in a classical modernist building such as Mies van der Rohe's National Gallery in Berlin, systematicity resists the ecological because the governing hierarchy of the constellation dictates a clear nesting and articulation of all constituents at all levels. Here, geometry has a regulatory function: defining, classifying and segregating spatial, programmatic and structural relations. This fixity breeds the classical harmonies, both formal and affective, of equilibrium and repose.

Lerner Hall equally employs hierarchy, but according to the logics of open systems rather than the closed systems of classicism. Thus, it is generative of states of imbalance and dynamics far from equilibrium. This is an architecture conditioned by a sensitive field of relations that run through all built scales, that are present, in varying degrees of influence, in all parts of the building. The interactions of these relations follow the pattern of the abstract machine as described by the philosopher Gilles Deleuze.[1] Here, the organization follows machinic pathways which are productive of degrees of freedom and constraint. On the one hand, the building's wings are perhaps overdetermined by historicist codes. On the other hand, its programmatic and material core is so refined as to register the most poised interactions. Indeed, at the level of structure and materials, we see conditions of extreme concentration where, as Hugh Dutton points out, the passing of scalar and material limits eliminates the secondary structure – as, for example, when glass itself absorbs the forces once taken up by secondary structural elements. Moreover, we see moments of delicate simplicity where a complex of forces bound within a structural assembly uncouple and are then distributed into individual components. Movements between simplicity and complexity are often linked, as when the multi-dimensional forces from the building's structure are absorbed by the ramps which, acting in conjunction with the curtain-wall assembly, separate them into simple forces by the time they reach the exterior glazing.

Inasmuch as the work of architects and engineers ultimately overlaps in the same material construct, their respective procedures already find expression in a common field. While architecture necessarily exceeds the parameters of engineering, the foregrounding of structural logics seen in Lerner Hall stems from the fact that they provide the most direct and literal index of forces in matter (even in typological models) and, thus, are sensitive enough to register the complex interplay of programme, structure and flows.[2]

In this regard, Lerner Hall signals a crucial turning point in Tschumi's oeuvre. While a legacy of built and unbuilt works beginning with The Manhattan Transcripts have prioritized the programmatic as an irreducible precondition to architecture, Lerner Hall inverts this logic, foregrounding physicality instead. Interestingly, programme seems to play even more intensively through this structured field than in former projects. This direction of work, however, has no aspirations towards innovative engineering as an isolated condition, but sees its participation within an extended field of influences. Increasingly, modernist paradigms, especially those that would seek to purify or reduce practices to a limited set of criteria (for example, when an engineer strives to find the most minimal structural solution, i.e. the purest tensile structure) by all evidence have reached their limit, and in all likelihood will be unable to produce new possibilities within the same constraints. This, then, is not a representation of engineering so as to manifest yet another engineering style, nor is it reducible to a modernist model of engineering that would seek to purify a spatial and material logic. Rather than a model of ultimate efficiency, it engenders an architecture of complex interactions, pragmatically and organizationally.

Finally, a conservative history could be advanced, ascribing lineage and influences to the various spatial and tectonic components of Lerner Hall. From the seminal work of figures like Le Corbusier, and his architecture promenade, to Norman Foster and Renzo Piano's valorizing of engineering, a plethora of lines can be drawn. Direct affiliations, even more compelling, given linked histories from the Arup organization under Peter Rice to Dutton and Tschumi, would complete this conservative lineage. However, there is another history less tied to seminal figures and canonical works – a mute history driven by confluences of politics, technique and desire. Such determinants arguably run through all the antecedents of Lerner Hall, yet in none have they coalesced in such a fundamentally different way. Lerner Hall does not emerge out of nothing, but its precedents, from the continuous ramps down to the components of curtain-walls, arrive not as models but as a mutable array charged with historical becoming. For this project is resonant not simply because it is a good building, or good of its kind, but because it occupies a signal position in fulfilling speculations of a generation that came before and in initiating unforeseen trajectories that point the way towards works to come.

Notes

[1] The French philosopher Gilles Deleuze coined the concept of the 'machinic phylum' to refer to the overall set of self-organizing processes in the universe. These include all processes in which a group of previously disconnected elements (organic and non-organic) suddenly reach a critical point at which they begin to 'cooperate' to form a higher-level entity. Recent advances in experimental mathematics have shown that the onset of these processes may be described by the same mathematical model. It is as if the principles that guide the self-assembly of these 'machines are at some deep level essentially similar'. The notion of a 'machinic phylum' thus blurs the distinction between organic and non-organic life.

[2] This type of systemic mixing is relatively new to architecture, though it is a standard practice in the field of industrial design (the design of a custom building component such as a curtain-wall system is arguably already a part of this field). For example, the mixture of components that comprise an automobile engine are conditioned by an array of competing limits. Theoretically, given unlimited space to expand, the parts of the engine might very well develop as an expanded grid of linked yet distinct entities. However, given the very real limits exerted on the one hand by the envelope (the extensive limit) and on the other by the necessary proximity of mechanical, chemical and electrical components (the intensive limits), a mediating assembly such as an engine block must accommodate and incorporate these intensive and extensive functions and influences. In doing so it moulds tightly around cylinders and crank shafts while sprouting numerous appendages and attachment points for the systems that feed these organs, all the while growing within a highly defined limit of the body shell.

Havemeyer   Mathematics   Earl Hall   Lewisohn   Dodge   Journalism   Furnald   CUSC

117th St.   116th St.   115th St.   114th St.

In the spring of 1994 Bernard Tschumi Architects were asked by the Trustees of Columbia University to participate in the redesign of a student centre for the campus.

Deviations from the Normative
Bernard Tschumi

The site of the project was the old Ferris Booth Hall, a centre for student activities built in 1958.

Over three decades, the building had fallen into disrepair and, more important, the needs and dynamics of student life had far outpaced its spaces and conceptual design. We elected to work with Gruzen Samton, who had undertaken the initial planning study for the site and had considerable experience with school facilities (notably the design of the prestigious Stuyvesant High School in Manhattan). It was assumed that, as Dean of the Graduate School of Architecture, Planning and Preservation at Columbia, I understood both student needs and the context of the project. In particular, the project fitted in with my own interest, spanning two decades of work, in the programmes, activities or events that take place in buildings and define their spaces.

It quickly became apparent that the current and future needs of students would not be met by an extension to or renovation of the existing building. The Trustees of Columbia and Columbia's President, George Rupp – aided by the generosity of a distinguished alumnus, Alfred Lerner – gave the go-ahead for the construction of a new 225,000 square-foot centre that would contain a 1,500-seat combined auditorium and assembly hall, three dining facilities, lounges, meeting rooms, a night club, bookstore, radio station, student clubs and games rooms, administrative spaces, a black box theatre and 6,000 mailboxes, as well as expanded computer facilities for student use. In response to the pattern of campus life, many of these facilities would operate twenty-four hours a day and be open to the surrounding community as a whole.

The context of the future building was a source of both inherent interest and difficulties. The corner site fronts Broadway and adjoins the Carman Hall dormitory on 114th Street. Upper Broadway is defined, on one side, by residential buildings, small stores and service facilities and, on the other, by the brick and granite materials and

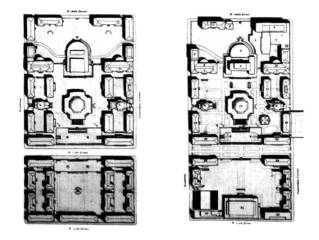

1870 master plan (left) and existing plan (right), with Alfred Lerner Hall bottom left

vocabulary of the construction developed by McKim, Mead and White for the Columbia campus in 1870. Recent preservation efforts have repeatedly threatened to landmark the Columbia campus, impeding future construction, yet the inner framework of the historical master plan is made up of broad open spaces, animated by the perpetual passage and activities of bodies — the stage for the dynamics of student life.

Because the student centre is linked both to Broadway and to the McKim master plan, and could be considered as a possible model for new buildings in the campus, we began by developing a general strategy.

a. In terms of the building's exterior, our urban hypothesis was to respect and even reinforce the spatial and volumetric logic of the master plan. Some of the original building materials, such as granite, brick and a copper-like material, would also be used.

b. Simultaneously, within this existing normative framework, we tried to provide an innovative programmatic space — a student city within the city of Columbia University (an urban focus reinforced by the relation of the university to the city of New York).

This two-pronged strategy could be summarized as 'a quiet building on the outside, a stimulating building on the inside'.

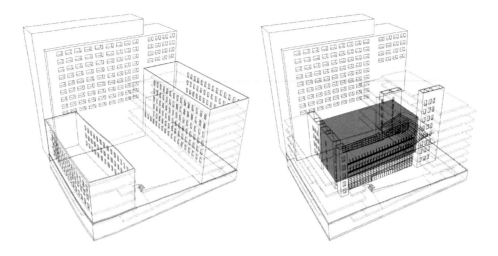

The Outside (The Normative)

The 1870 master plan shows a pairing of the buildings parallel to Broadway and Amsterdam Avenue. Only one of these double buildings — Avery Hall — was ever built. For the new student centre, we suggested a strategy that works within the regulating volumetric lines of the original plan, exploiting its potential for an internal densification of the campus. We placed the required functional rooms within the double rectangular volumes, namely a Broadway wing and a campus wing, and set large public spaces, such as the main lobby, auditorium and theatre, in the void between the two. The wings use materials prevalent in the historical campus, while the space between them is as transparent as the most advanced technology allows.

The eight-storey Broadway wing contains a 400-seat cinema and assembly hall, games areas, student administration, student clubs, a bookstore and radio station, with three floors of potential academic/administrative spaces. The cinema screen can be folded so that the space can act as a balcony to the auditorium. In terms of its visual presence, the Broadway block extends the theme of the Columbia street front — a patterned brick facade over a granite base.

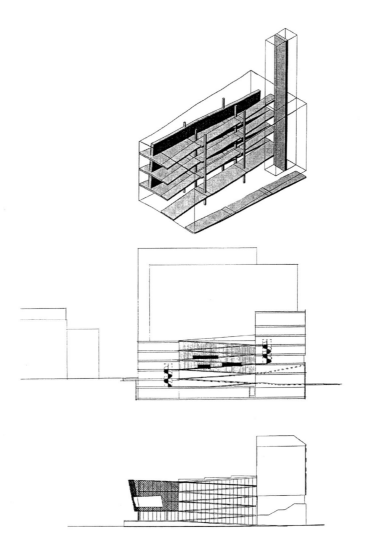

The four-storey campus wing includes the main entrance, a twenty-four-hour area, dining services, a night club (The Plex) and meeting rooms.

One specific site feature also demanded attention in the development of the scheme. The eastern, Broadway side is one full half-floor lower than the western, campus level, which suggested an inherent contradiction in the Beaux-Arts logic of the McKim, Mead and White scheme. Could we turn this topographical condition to our advantage?

The In-between (The Exception or Deviation)

If a normative context was the strategy for the outside, invention was our aim for the building interior. While the old Ferris Booth Hall provided neither a breathing space nor an overview of its different uses, Lerner Hall is designed to act as a forum, a dynamic place of exchange. The centre could be described as a hub, the major social space for the student body. Its varied activities are to be perceived from the series of oblique lounges – suspended glass ramps – that link the multiplicity of disparate functions into a new university event.

The ramps provide the main circulatory system for the building, tying together lobbies and student lounges, information stands, mailboxes, locations for exhibitions or student propaganda, and accommodating overspill from other activities – bar, games and so forth. The ramps respond to the topographical condition of the campus. As opposed to conventional atrium spaces – which would be surrounded by full floors stacked every twelve feet – the floors on the campus and Broadway sides are staggered half-floors, located every six feet and linked by simple ramps. Hence the building hallways act as a continuous link between what would normally be discontinuous and even contradictory activities; they are simultaneously a void and a route – a space of exchange and a place of passage. During the day, light filters through the glass ramps, and the broad expanse of the Columbia campus is visible through the 100 foot by 50 foot interconnected glass wall. At night, as light glows from the inside, figures in movement along this route appear as if in a silent shadow theatre.

The project was also intended to deviate from the normative in its use of exceptional technology to implement its programmatic aims. It adopts dimensions of glass previously unused in the United States, and its intersupporting frames of ramps and walls are creative interventions in the field of engineering. The context into which the innovative event of the glass wall and ramps inserts itself is that of the traditional (generally resistant) New York construction industry, whose methods have changed little since the time of McKim. However, Lerner Hall is also a polemic, a building that will undoubtedly be attacked by critics from the right and from the left, by conservatives as well as by progressives. Conservatives will condemn its transparent glass expanse as heresy within the historical context of the Columbia campus. Progressives will decry its use of granite, bricks and cornice as a disgrace to progress and newness. Some may question the relevance of the new, computer-driven technology used in fabricating the glass wall, since it contradicts more conventional building techniques employed elsewhere in the building. Both conservatives and progressives may view the building as a compromise.

Our intention, however, was to design a building which is simultaneously generic and specific, which does not adhere to one singular (and signature) style, aesthetic or sensibility. We made the building simultaneously the norm and the exception. Columbia University had requested that we follow the Flemish-bond brick pattern of the historical McKim, Mead and White buildings. We did not object to McKim's law, much as one does not object to driving on the left while in England. What interested us specifically were the interstices in the law, the eccentric and productive allowances, the gap between the two McKim solids indicated in the master plan.

Moreover, our point was that neither the normative nor the exceptional was to be about form. We avoided designing this building in the compositional sense, i.e. vertically or horizontally, fragmented or continuous, projecting or receding, using sculptural or minimalist, abstract or figurative shapes. Architecture, as approached in this project, is seen as the materialization of a concept rather than the materialization of form. Whilst you cannot avoid the use of forms as you build – ultimately everything has a material form – the materialization of concepts leads to carefully developed technologies rather than to imagistic assemblages of shapes. Hence the two solids in Lerner Hall follow the normative framework of McKim, while the ramps use the tensile capabilities of contemporary glass and steel.

Early Sketches

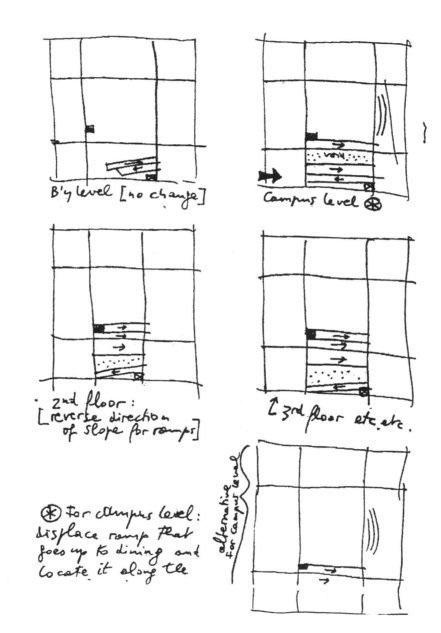

B'y level [no change]

Campus level ✸

2nd floor:
[reverse direction of slope for ramps]

↳ 3rd floor etc. etc.

alternative for campus level

✸ for campus level: displace ramp that goes up to dining and locate it along the

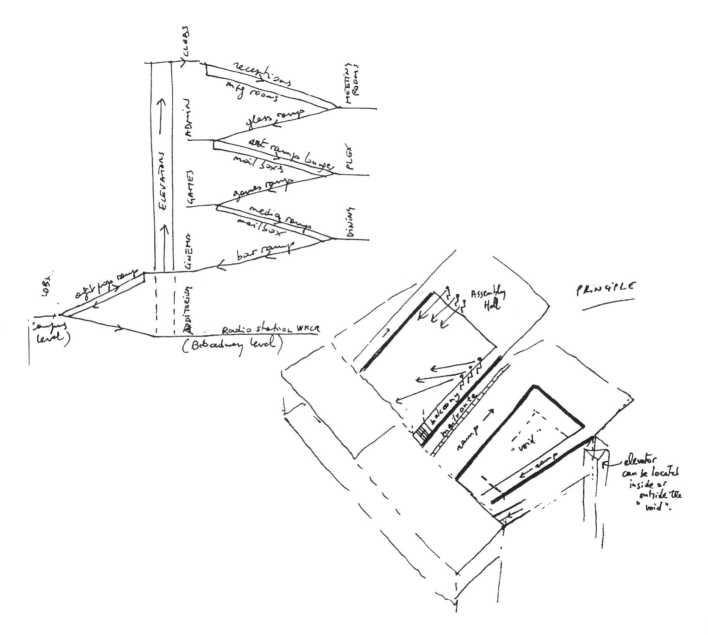

CLUBS

receptions

mtg rooms

MEETING ROOMS

glass ramp

ADMIN

art ramp lounge

mail boxs

PLGK

games ramp

GAMES

media ramp

mailbox

DINING

ELEVATORS

bar ramp

CINEMA

LOBY

apt yoga ramp

(camping level)

AUDITORIUM

Radio station WKCR

(Broadway level)

Assembly Hall

balcony

balcony ramp

ramp

"void"

ramp

PRINCIPLE

elevator can be located inside or outside the "void".

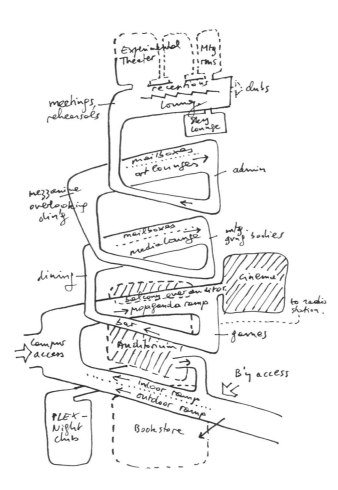

8/94

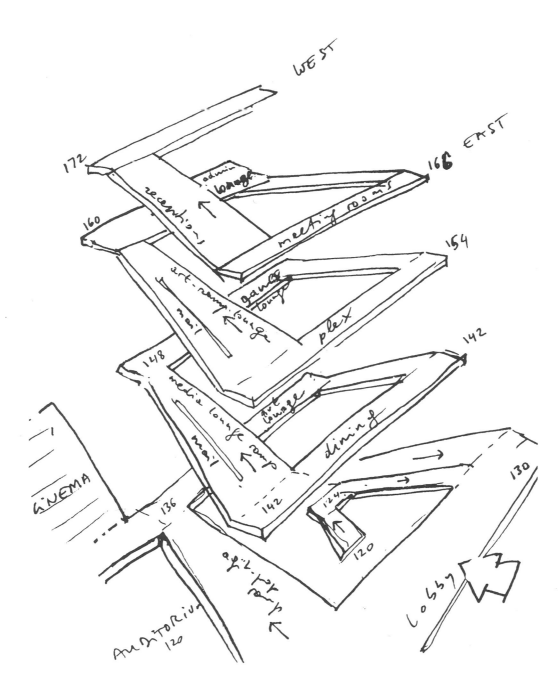

WEST

EAST

172

166

160

reception

admin lounge

meeting rooms

154

art-ramp lounge

games lounge

mail

plex

148

media lounge

art lounge

142

mail

ramp

dining

142

124

130

CINEMA

136

120

Lobby

art-dept ramp

AUDITORIUM
120

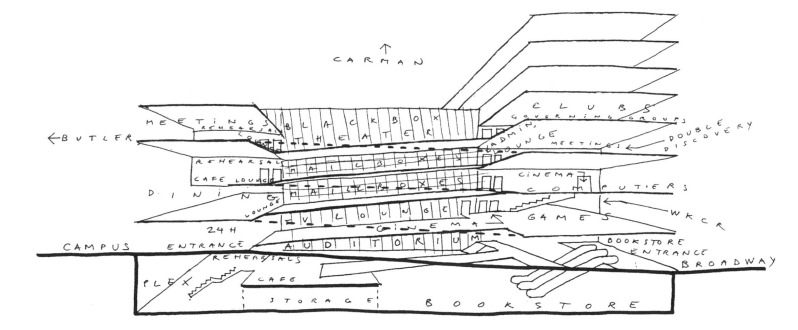

CARMAN

CLUBS
GOVERNING GROUPS
MEETINGS &
REHEARSALS   BLACK BOX   THEATER   DOUBLE
MEETINGS   ADMIN.   DISCOVERY
← BUTLER   LOUNGE   MEETINGS
REHEARSALS   MAILBOXES
CAFE LOUNGE   CINEMA
                                                  COMPUTERS
DINING   MAILBOXES
            LOUNGE   GAMES   WKCR
            TV LOUNGE
        24 H   CINEMA
CAMPUS ENTRANCE   AUDITORIUM   BOOKSTORE
                                              ENTRANCE
                                                      BROADWAY
PLEX   REHEARSALS
            CAFE
            STORAGE   BOOKSTORE

30

Front Elevation:

'Conservative' version.

west. Elev:

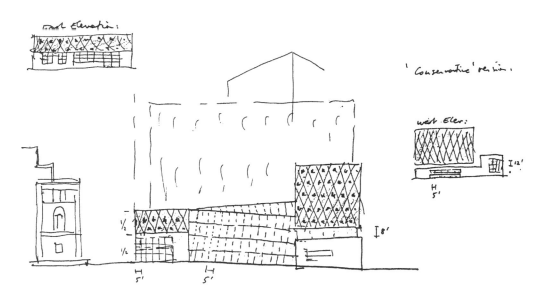

I 12'

H 5'

1/2

1/2

I 8'

H 5'

H 5'

7-24-94

'advanced' version.

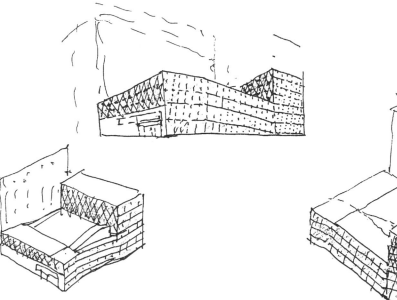

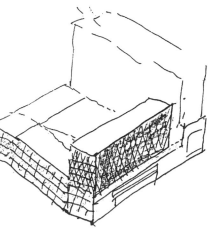

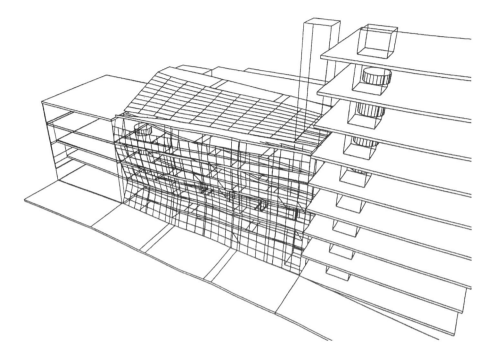

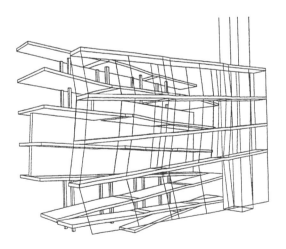

Glass Ramps

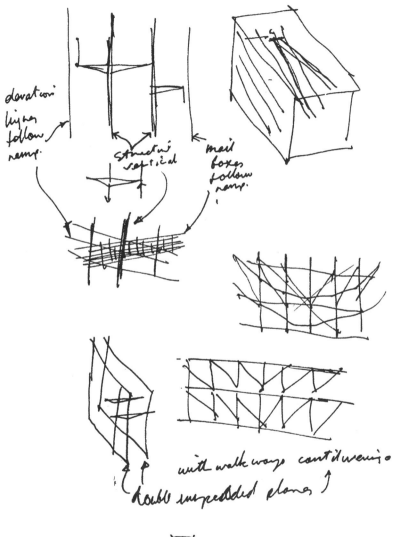

elevation
lines
follow
ramp.

Structure
vertical

mail
boxes
follow
ramp.

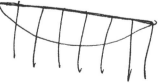

with walkways cantilevering

double suspended planes ↑

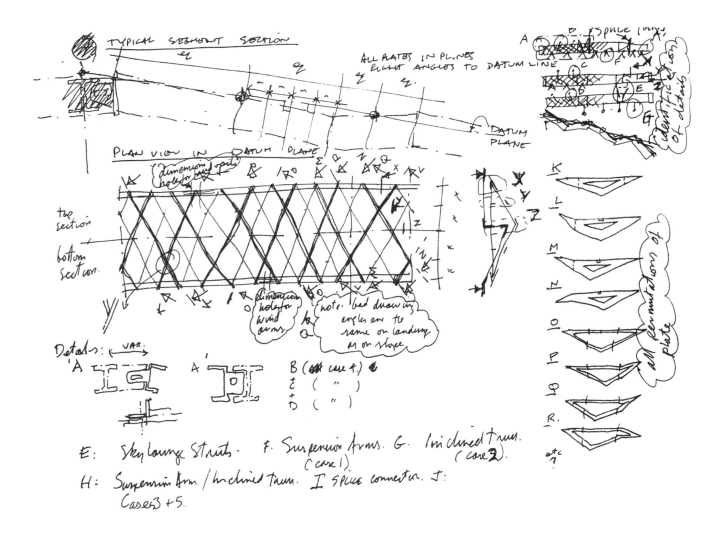

TYPICAL SEGMENT SECTION

ALL PLATES IN PLANES
RIGHT ANGLES TO DATUM LINE

DATUM
PLANE

PLAN VIEW IN DATUM PLANE

dimension
hole for hand rail

top
section

bottom
section.

dimension
hole for
wind
arms.

note: bad drawing
angles are the
same on landing
as on slope

A SPLICE JOINT

identification of details

K
L
M
N
O
P
Q
R
etc
?

all permutations of plate

Details: VAR.

'A'   A'   B (all case 4.)
                                  C   (")
                                  + D (")

E: Sky lounge Struts.   F. Suspension Arms.   G. Inclined Truss.
                            (case 1.)   (case 2).

H: Suspension Arm / Inclined Truss.   I space connector.   J:
      Cases 3 + 5.

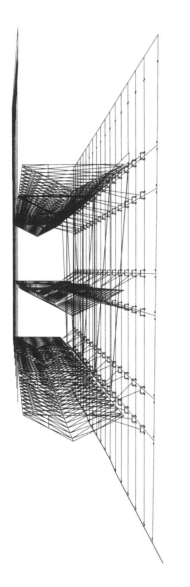

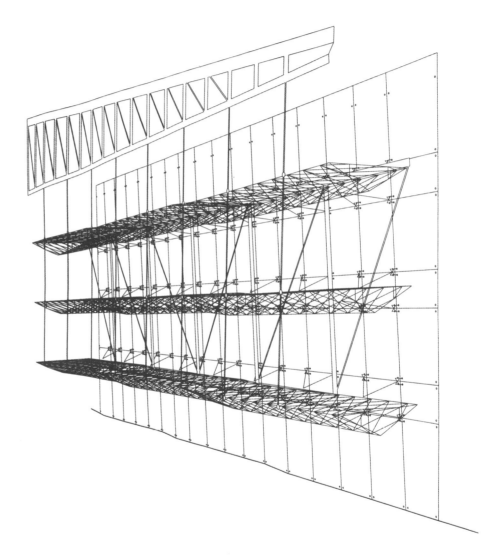

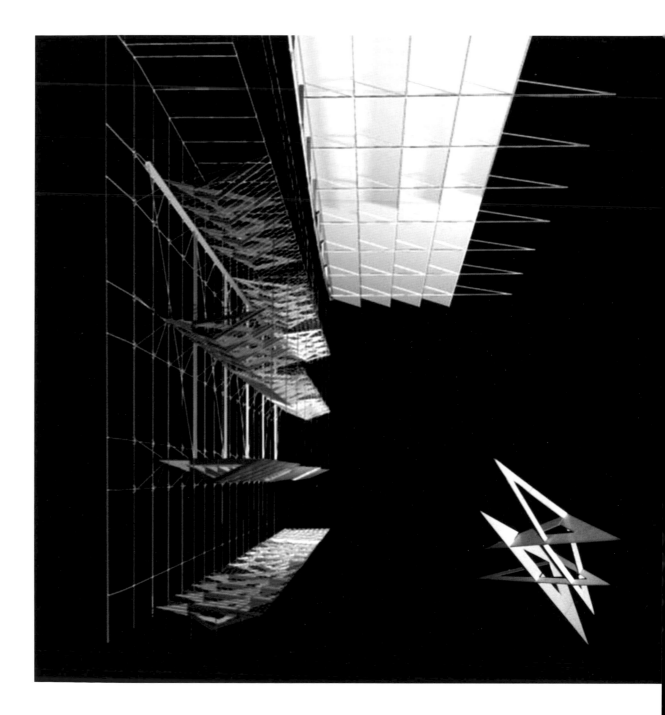

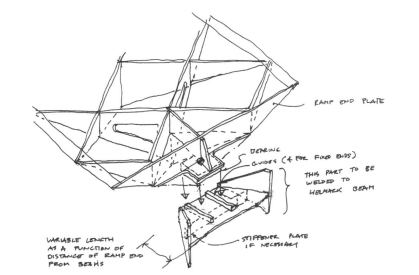

RAMP END PLATE

BEARING
GUIDES (4 FOR FIXED ENDS)

THIS PART TO BE
WELDED TO
HELMACK BEAM

VARIABLE LENGTH
AS A FUNCTION OF
DISTANCE OF RAMP END
FROM BEAMS

STIFFENER PLATE
IF NECESSARY

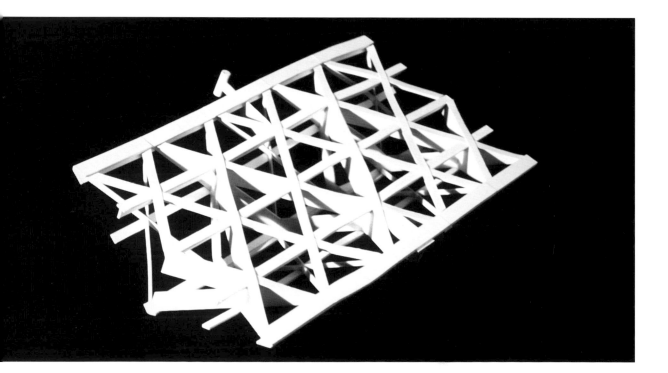

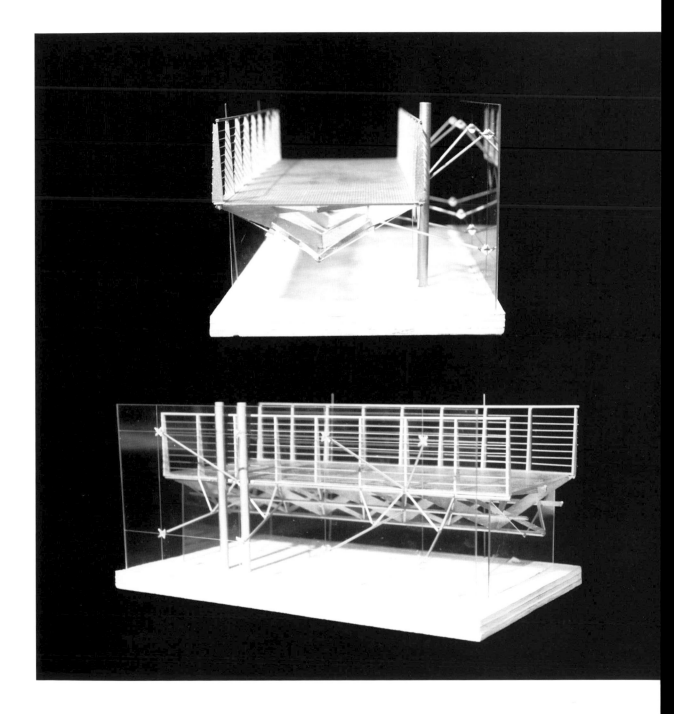

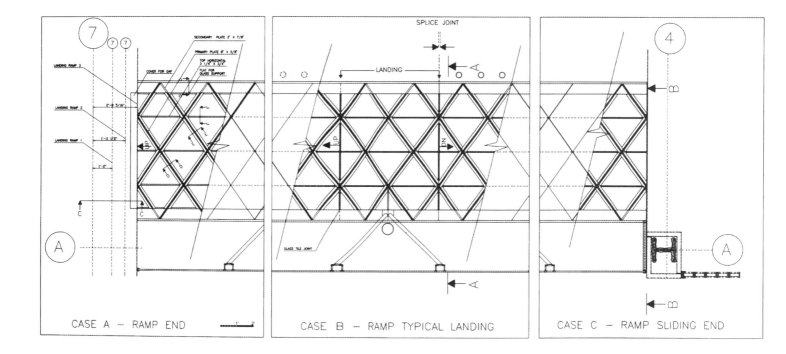

SPLICE JOINT

SECONDARY PLATE 2" X 7/8"

PRIMARY PLATE 6" X 5/8"

TOP HORIZONTAL
3 1/4" X 3/4"

FLAT FOR
GLASS SUPPORT

COVER FOR GAP

LANDING RAMP 3

LANDING RAMP 2

LANDING RAMP 1

LANDING

GLASS TILE JOINT

CASE A — RAMP END

CASE B — RAMP TYPICAL LANDING

CASE C — RAMP SLIDING END

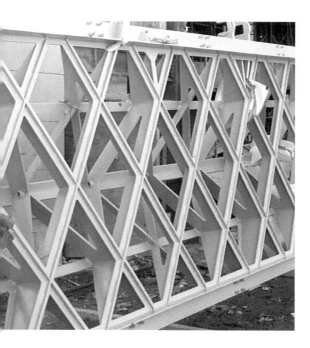

Roof Transfer Truss

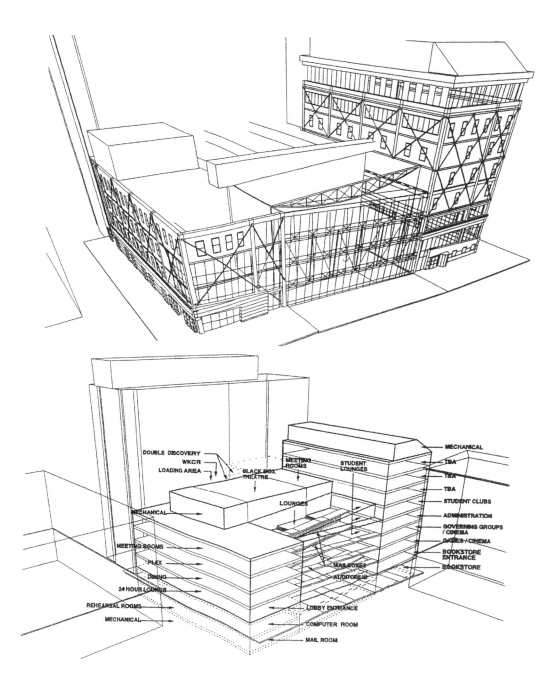

DOUBLE DISCOVERY
WKCR
LOADING AREA
BLACK BOX THEATRE
MEETING ROOMS
STUDENT LOUNGES
MECHANICAL
TBA
TBA
TBA
STUDENT CLUBS
ADMINISTRATION
GOVERNING GROUPS / CINEMA
GAMES / CINEMA
BOOKSTORE ENTRANCE
BOOKSTORE
MECHANICAL
LOUNGES
MEETING ROOMS
PLEX
DINING
24 HOUR LOUNGE
REHEARSAL ROOMS
MECHANICAL
MAIL BOXES
AUDITORIUM
LOBBY ENTRANCE
COMPUTER ROOM
MAIL ROOM

46

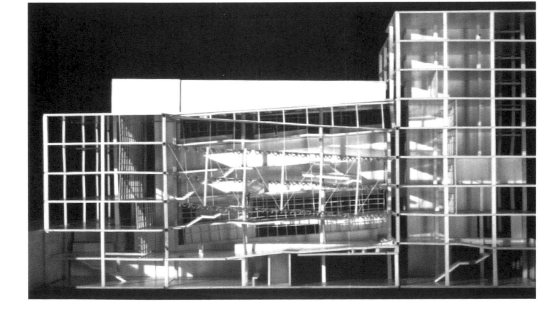

With a clearly visible steel structure and glass surfaces, the glass wall and supporting ramps in Lerner Hall provide a transparent counterpoint to the two masonry-clad wings on either side. The struc-

Muddling the Boundaries
Hugh Dutton

wings on either side. The structure spans these blocks and the glass encloses the hub void between them. The articulation of the trusses and ramp steel expresses the activity and movement zone of the hub itself. The structural components – ramp wind beams, main trellis truss, suspension rods and cantilevered glass support arms – all animate the space. The inclined arrangement of the ramps and trusses is a logical consequence of the change in level between the street at Broadway and the main campus, which is half a typical floor above it. This angular geometry is carried through the layout of all the components of the facade and the ramps – the glass grid follows the incline of the ramps, as do all the support arms and fixing brackets.

The elevation is composed through the superposition of individual structural elements or glass support parts, each with a different geometry, volume and texture. The inclined facade truss (IFT) is a simple triangulated trellis beam with tubes as compression members and rod ties as tension members. This truss partially supports the ramps, which are an intricate mesh of diagonally assembled plates. The inner edges of the ramps are suspended by a virtual plane of inclined ties from another, much heavier, triangulated trellis truss at roof level. Each of these structural components is transparent in one way or another. The glass wall, with its own inclined matrix of joints, is fixed to the ramps with cantilever arms arranged as a series of X points punctuating the elevation.

The glass is used structurally. Each panel supports its own dead weight and wind loads. The absence of glazing bars or mullions creates a pure, transparent, weatherproof glass surface that is clearly distinct from the steel structure. Walking surfaces on the ramps are also made of glass, in the form of laminated tiles. The upper sheet of tiles is toughened and covered in an anti-slip treatment (a dust of tiny glass beads,

51

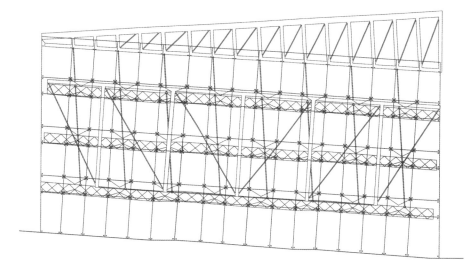

vitrified to the surface). Extensive tests established the impact resistance of the ramps and their capacity to prevent objects from penetrating their surface, in the event of accidental breakage.

Lerner Hall is the first application in the United States of the articulated point-fixing glazing system developed in the early 1980s by Peter Rice's team at Parc de la Villette in Paris. The system is based on bolts with a spherical bearing in their heads, allowing a movement-free connection between the glass and its fixings. The project is conceived in the same spirit as La Villette – as a visual expression of the critical functional details. Each detail is designed to demonstrate how it works.

Each cantilever X arm consists of two lower gravity arms that support the dead weight of the glass, and 'wind' arms that support wind loads only. This configuration provides a clear analysis of how the glass will behave structurally, and guarantees that it can only be loaded in the manner for which it is designed. Each lite is simply and independently supported, and any relative movement between the arms or between the ramps cannot be transferred into the glass as a load, a concept rigorously carried through all of the details. In the case of the gravity arms, one lite is suspended from a cast end bracket, and the other rests on it. In the case of the wind arms, the end bracket is used to fix a group of small articulated struts that can resist wind loads perpendicular to the glass plane but are free to rotate in all other directions. This guarantees that they cannot resist any forces in the plane of the glass. If, for example, the weight of a crowd of people causes the upper ramp to deflect downwards, then the lite suspended from it is free to move slightly downwards without pushing on the arm of the ramp below it. This principle is crucial in terms of the composition because it allows the glass to be fixed to each ramp independently and directly, without any secondary framing (as would probably have been the case in a conventional glazing application).

The arms are hung from the ramps via a system of turnbuckles so that construction tolerances can be corrected even when the glass is in place. This allows for any fine-tuning that may be necessary once the whole system has settled under the dead weight of the glass. The castings themselves are also equipped with adjustment devices for fine-tuning and, in particular, for angular correction to compensate for differences in arm angles. A spherical bearing at the core of each piece permits rotation. These adjustment devices also enable the correction of any slight non-alignment of the ramp slope landings, as required by New York City building codes. The castings are important components of the design because they resolve, within a single piece, the problems resulting from the geometric complexity of the building. The cast fabrication technique allows an almost total freedom of shape. It gives these key parts a unique identity specific to this project, allowing them to express, in an almost sculptural manner, the resolution of the overall geometric composition at a hand-sized scale.

The actual casting process began with three-dimensional computer modelling. The models were then transmitted directly to the tool-and-die manufacturer to be made into moulds. We used the lost-wax casting technique, whereby the mould tool is used to make a wax version of the piece, which in turn is coated to make a strong ceramic shell. The wax is then melted out of the shell and replaced with a pour of molten stainless steel. After grit-blasting, the piece is machined for the necessary bolting and threading connections.

In engineering terms, although the main components (with the exception of the ramps) are simple and classic structural elements, their movements and interaction required careful analysis. This analysis, conducted by Ove Arup's New York office, included the use of three-dimensional electronic models to evaluate the interactive behaviour of the different structural components and, in particular, the relative stiffness of the two different trusses and the ramps that they support. Arup's structural design included the precision engineering of all the steel details according to New York City and general American design standards. A full verification re-analysis was then conducted in a peer review by Wiedlinger, another New York engineering firm.

The ramps themselves are of a complex geometry, and a full volumetric analysis was required to understand the structural capacity of the tight mesh of small elements from which they are constructed. Every piece of steel in the ramps is fully exploited, both for its structural capacity and as a supporting element for secondary finishes or cladding items (such as handrails, glass support arms, glass floor tiling, etc.). The glass flooring can be paved directly onto the main structure and has no secondary framing. Indeed, there is no such thing as secondary structure or framing – everything is primary.

Such an intricate interface between traditionally distinct construction trades required a particular contractual arrangement. To ensure the necessary coordination, the designers proposed that one contractor should take full responsibility for all components of the glass wall and steel ramp design, and that all of it should be let under a single bid package. Given that this type of construction is not common in the United States (and is particularly uncommon in New York City), it was recommended that the job be opened to tenders from abroad. The selection of candidates was made even more complicated by the fact that the building industry in New York has very particular regulations and customs. Three different European firms (teamed up with local partners) were ultimately consulted, along with the only American firm with a proven track record in this kind of construction. The willingness of a broad range of

companies to undertake the project raised confidence in the feasibility of implementing such unfamiliar technology.

All contractors were asked to submit pre-tender prices for the work, with a view to establishing budgetary feasibility and a confirmation of the construction manager's Guaranteed Maximum Price (GMP). This process was followed by a full tender, which was won by the French firm Eiffel, in partnership with New Jersey Windows and Precision Specialist Metal and Glass Inc., for the on-site erection.

To resolve the complications arising from a European steel company working in New York using European product standards and measurement systems, significant cooperation was required from all concerned. Beyond the issue of standards, there was a separate cultural barrier to be overcome – the tried-and-tested methods, practices and conventions of contractual responsibility in one local construction industry diverge from those in other countries. Different time zones and language barriers added further challenges to simple communication.

Under the terms of its contract Eiffel was to produce an engineering reanalysis and detailed shop drawings for approval by Arup and the design team. Following this phase, a mock-up of the typical components of glazing and ramp steel was fabricated in France and shipped to New York for review. The prototype helped the local crews to familiarize themselves with the glazing technology and provided a trial run for the erection.

Different components of the work were sourced from an almost bewildering number of places, partly because of their specificity, and partly because of Eiffel's existing commercial contacts. The steel was fabricated in Alsace, in Eiffel's Mezières facility near Metz. The glass tiles for the ramps were made at Saint-Gobain in the Paulliac region near Bordeaux, an area better known for its wine than for glass. The vertical glass, although made at the Saint-Gobain glassworks, was cut, machined and treated in Villa Franca, near Venice, Italy. Although it would have had obvious practical advantages in terms of replacement and transportation, the glass could not have been economically produced in the United States, because the heat-soak testing procedure for foreign body inclusions in tempered glass is not common local practice. (The test is a destructive one in which glass is reheated to 290°C and shatters if any imperfections occur.)

Precision Specialist Metal and Glass Inc.'s New York team erected the steel and the glass. Each ramp segment was erected on scaffolding staging and welded on site. The main inclined facade truss (IFT) was assembled entirely on the ground and erected in a single lift on 12 May 1998, using a huge telescopic crane. Once the IFT was in place, the ramp ties were connected, the suspension ties attached and the ramp scaffolding removed. At this point the structure began to perform as it was designed to, spanning the space between the two wings of the building. Glass erection followed after a detailed survey of the position of all of the cast arm bolt brackets. Despite adjustment difficulties on site (the tolerance errors added up and manifested themselves in the last element of the puzzle to be put together), all the glass was set and sealed with silicone sealant. The glazing system of Lerner Hall was complete.

Inclined Facade Truss

Bernard Tschumi: When we've talked about the various ways architects, designers and engineers work, we've sometimes made analogies with the film industry. The

Conversation between
Bernard Tschumi and Hugh Dutton

role of architects is open to interpretation. They can aspire to be the 'star' – an actor, constructing their own persona – or they can be more like the director – giving overall coherence to a work which is produced by a large number of people with their own distinct areas of expertise. Personally, I believe that architecture is about ideas and concepts, and not simply about forms that twist, collide or go bump in the night. I also think that if you are pushing an architectural concept as far as you can, you should attempt to achieve a level of technological innovation – the most important part of the concept should also be technologically the most inventive. Historically, architects have produced some of their most significant work by pushing technology to its next stage. And you don't do that by yourself.

To help develop the concept you need a number of people with a broad range of expertise. As in a film, you need to put together a team, because architecture is not simply the translation into technical terms of a seductive drawing. For the more conventional areas of Lerner Hall, we worked in a creative way with fairly 'straight' engineers and the Gruzen Samton office; for the ramps, we worked with yourself and Ove Arup. The respective team compositions reflect the difference between the normative and the exceptional, and the specialist competences of these different people take the concept one step further. It's not just technology per se, it's architecture pushed to its limits. Through technology.

Hugh Dutton: In the building profession a distinction is generally made between the architect and the engineer (and, in the United States, the curtain-wall cladding consultant). I don't know if this sort of barrier exists in the film industry, but in the architectural field people are obsessed with liability. They draw clear protective lines around their individual zones of activity, in order to define what they are and aren't responsible for – what they can or can't be sued for. But if, as you're saying, one wants to push a project forward technologically (and thus reap the highest dividends architecturally) it is best to muddle these boundaries. The architecture, the engineering and the curtain-wall consultancy can then be considered in a much more integrated, and integral, way. They're no longer different disciplines.

BT: I think this is very important, insofar as it concerns what's required from the various people involved in the project. As an architect, you need to have a relative understanding of the capabilities of each of the different domains that make up the building process – the glass manufacturer, the mason, or whatever. You need to know how far you can push them, so they will not only do everything they are capable of, but also, perhaps, redefine in some way their 'individual' area of competence. As an illustration, I could use a revealing exchange that took place during our own collaboration on the French National Library competition in 1989. In my New York office we had developed a series of circuits, including a running track, that we wanted to 'hover' over the rest of the library. We sent a fax to you in Paris describing the problem and quite quickly we got your first proposal showing a straightforward series of columns – which was the most reasonable thing to do. I faxed back, saying that it seemed a little pedestrian. And within a few hours you came up with an absolutely amazing sketch showing angled supports that looked a bit like those 1950s Festival of Britain skylons (or 'cigars' as we later called them). I could understand the skylon thing right away, but because of the different angles there was something about the system that seemed inherently unstable. While I certainly liked it, I felt it would never hold. I sent a fax back to you: 'You're nuts! It's gonna crash!'

HD: You mentioned, at the time, that Peter Rice had given a lecture at Columbia called 'Unstable Structures'.

BT: Right. Peter was always rushed, and didn't have time to give us a title – so I invented one for him. When he arrived and saw the title he said, 'If engineers created unstable structures, we'd be put in jail right away. But let me try to rise to the occasion and discuss the theme that's been proposed: what it means to have stable structures that don't look stable, but…'

HD: … are true to structural forces.

BT: That's correct, structures that play with tension and compression in a novel way. For the French National Library competition it was important, architecturally, to emphasize the dynamism of the concept at that particular point of the structure. That's why the exchange between our respective teams was crucial.

HD: I remember the same to-ing and fro-ing with the Lerner Hall glass ramps. There are two 'halfway landings' on the ramps, which in the first drawings had columns underneath them – nice reasonable columns, coming down to the ground. At a later stage in the project, they disappeared. (I remember some Columbia official observing, 'Didn't we have columns here?'.) If the point is to push the concept to excess, then thank goodness they're not there. I was responding to the architectural concept when I suggested that we have a beam spanning the whole hundred-feet distance between the two 'McKim' blocks. For me, this was a structural manifestation of what the architecture was doing: you had the two McKim blocks on either side and the glass in between – it wasn't 'ramps sitting on columns'. The most important aspect of the final project is that you feel the transparency and apparent weightlessness of the glass. The idea to suspend the glass was, I think, a turning point in the project.

BT: That's because it allowed us to take advantage of the structural depth provided by three glass ramps. In other words, the twelve feet separating one ramp from the next would add up to twenty-four feet, which gave sufficient depth to span the hundred-foot gap between the two brick wings required by the McKim master plan. Anything that allowed the structure not to touch the ground was pushing the concept one step further. We had already discussed a maximum transparency for the glass and had many conversations about double-glazing versus single-glazing and having the ramp made out of glass plate. We had also spent a lot of time with the rest of the team reinforcing the 'banality' of the brick wings, as a foil to the 'exceptional' glass ramps.

HD: The ramps support the glazing, which is cantilevered off from them, so the entire wall plane depends on the ramps themselves. The ramps are also wind trusses: they span the hundred feet and take the wind load. We've designed parts of the structure to fulfil more than one purpose, which I think is crucial. When I spoke earlier about muddling the boundaries between professions, it was in reference to this kind of thing – an approach that engineers, with their analytical view of the structure, wouldn't necessarily think about. There's an integral attitude evident here, which is an important part of the building concept.

Another important issue in the design of the structure is the nature of the structural members themselves. In New York conventional steel construction uses beams – I-beams, H-beams, cruciform sections, or conventional laminated sections. We made a conscious decision not to use those sections in the key parts of the ramps because we wanted to allow them their individuality. So we have tubes and ties within the truss as either compression or tension members. Furthermore, these read very clearly as thick tubes and thin ties, to show the way the truss is working.

The ramp itself is a very complex resolution of forces coming from all sorts of directions – the performance of the ramp to form the truss, the performance to take the load of people walking on them, the performance to withstand the bending when you push on the handrail, where it's picked up by the suspension rods, or where the glass actually cantilevers off from it... Because of all these factors, the ramp is loaded in a very complex way, and we decided that the best way to respond to this complexity was to create a sort of mesh of criss-crossing plates, so that a single architectural configuration (the lattice) would resolve all the forces coming from every direction. The whole structure was clarified and made readable by having the mesh at a small scale and the truss at a much larger scale. Each element or structural component was clearly identifiable.

BT: There is another side to this. There are a number of conversations taking place on the architectural scene which involve a dialogue with other areas of culture (including philosophy or mathematics) and which challenge, or even propose erasing, the idea of hierarchy. We've tried to contribute to this discussion. We've shown that you can question and rearrange, but never completely erase. You could certainly say that we have questioned the respective roles of steel and glass, making them work with one another in a very contemporary way.

The idea of 'structural glass' is extremely interesting. Consider the implications of the name: normally glass is not structural, but fragile, so what level of autonomy can glass have without being held simply by mullions? At one point in the project – in a 'value engineering' session – we were asked to redesign the hall with columns and mullions. We duly prepared drawings showing what the project would look like, from the inside and the outside, with these heavy (but realistic) mullions...

HD: ... But that kind of re-working would have gone against the whole concept of the project. I think the success of the design is evident in the way that there is no vertical structure visible as you look horizontally along and across the ramps. You see only the five tubes of the outer truss and the suspension rods on the inside.

BT: The vertical tubes of the outer truss have almost the same diameter as the upper and lower compression members, which gives it a certain lightness.

HD: We called this the 'ghost truss' in our preliminary discussions, because a truss is much more efficient when it's deep. And here the truss is thirty-feet-deep, which means that there is very little load going through the members (although these still have to be a certain size, since the truss spans a hundred feet). Having said that, the issue is one of relative size and scale. If you compare the muscularity of the standard truss above with the ramp truss, the difference in how the span is perceived becomes obvious.

BT: Let's stay on this point for a moment. One of the crucial things in the design was to avoid holding the ramp symmetrically. To someone walking along the ramp, the left and the right sides should not appear to use the same structural system. The intention was to show a series of increasingly 'densified' layers leading finally to the other set of ramps – the fairly conventional concrete ramps of the TV lounge, mailbox system and auditorium – so that they read as a series of layers, but are all different. That asymmetry plays an incredibly important role in producing the dynamism of the ramp spaces.

HD: Another small point. Obviously, suspension rods are the most ethereal way to support something, but the other thing we did was to make the geometry of those internal rods follow the angle of the concrete ramps on the other side. This involves a geometrical shift which, again, clearly disconnects those ramps and suspension rods from the outer ramp system. We liked the idea, which goes right back to the Parc de la Villette,[1] an architecture composed with readable structural figures. A truss is a conventional configuration, it has a longitudinal beam, a diagonal tie. People recognize it as having a structural purpose. For the aluminium bridges along the east–west gallery at La Villette, we consciously used identifiable truss-figures – textbook examples of straight, curved and triangular trusses. We didn't try to sweep the structure under the carpet. It was part of the system. We were spanning between A and B.

BT: Much of architecture is about opposing, or 'confronting', the textbook features – what I call the normative – with the exceptional. It's the confrontation between the two that is important. I like designing with a tension between the banal and the unusual. But that would be another conversation...

[1] Hugh Dutton collaborated with Peter Rice and Bernard Tschumi on the main engineering features of Parc de la Villette.

Glass Wall

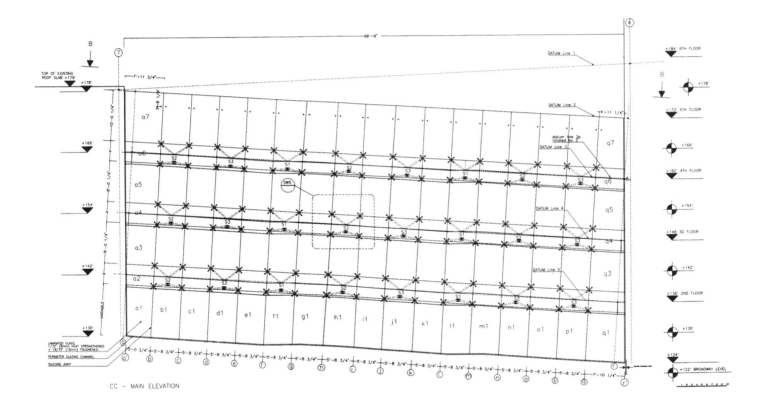

CC — MAIN ELEVATION

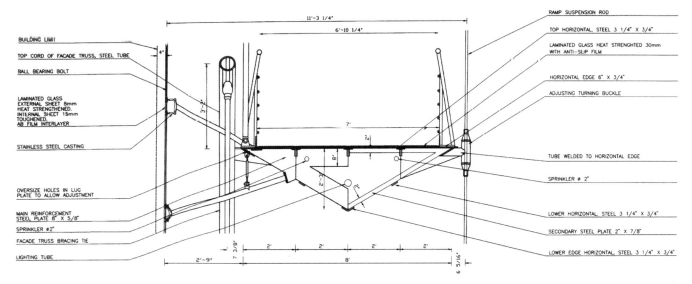

BUILDING LIMIT

TOP CORD OF FACADE TRUSS, STEEL TUBE

BALL BEARING BOLT

LAMINATED GLASS
EXTERNAL SHEET 8mm
HEAT STRENGHTENED.
INTERNAL SHEET 15mm
TOUGHENED.
AB FILM INTERLAYER

STAINLESS STEEL CASTING

OVERSIZE HOLES IN LUG
PLATE TO ALLOW ADJUSTMENT

MAIN REINFORCEMENT
STEEL PLATE 8" X 5/8"

SPRINKLER Ø2"

FACADE TRUSS BRACING TIE

LIGHTING TUBE

RAMP SUSPENSION ROD

TOP HORIZONTAL, STEEL 3 1/4" X 3/4"

LAMINATED GLASS HEAT STRENGHTED 30mm
WITH ANTI-SLIP FILM

HORIZONTAL EDGE 6" X 3/4"

ADJUSTING TURNING BUCKLE

TUBE WELDED TO HORIZONTAL EDGE

SPRINKLER Ø 2"

LOWER HORIZONTAL, STEEL 3 1/4" X 3/4"

SECONDARY STEEL PLATE 2" X 7/8"

LOWER EDGE HORIZONTAL, STEEL 3 1/4" X 3/4"

SECTION A-A - ARM CONNECTION TO RAMP

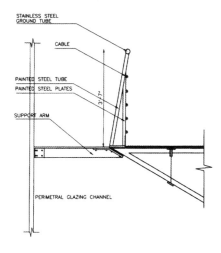

STAINLESS STEEL
GROUND TUBE

CABLE

PAINTED STEEL TUBE
PAINTED STEEL PLATES

SUPPORT ARM

PERIMETRAL GLAZING CHANNEL

SECTION B-B RAMP SLIDING END

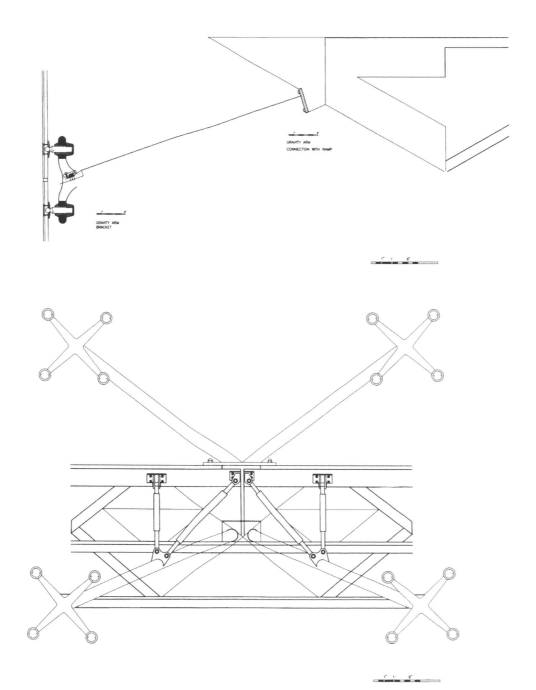

GRAVITY ARM
CONNECTION WITH RAMP

GRAVITY ARM
BRACKET

1" 1" 6"

1" 1" 6"

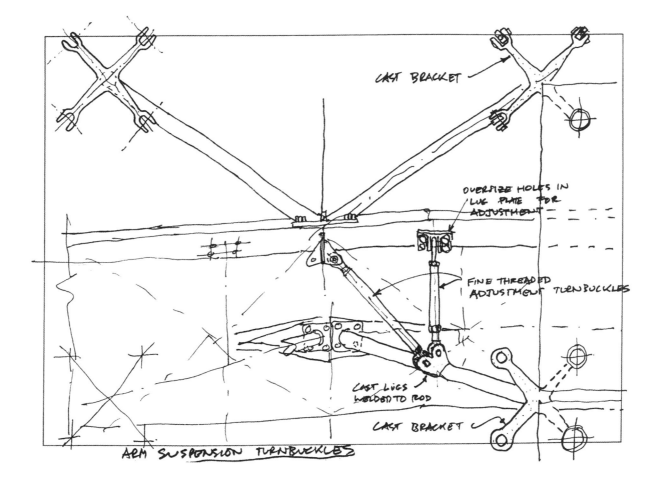

CAST BRACKET

OVERSIZE HOLES IN LUG PLATE FOR ADJUSTMENT

FINE THREADED ADJUSTMENT TURNBUCKLES

CAST LUGS WELDED TO ROD

CAST BRACKET

ARM SUSPENSION TURNBUCKLES

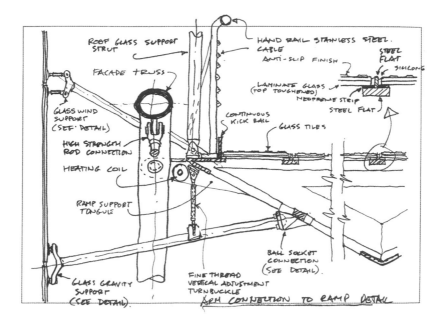

ROOF GLASS SUPPORT STRUT

FACADE TRUSS

GLASS WIND SUPPORT (SEE DETAIL)

HIGH STRENGTH ROD CONNECTION

HEATING COIL

RAMP SUPPORT TONGUE

GLASS GRAVITY SUPPORT (SEE DETAIL)

HAND RAIL STAINLESS STEEL. CABLE ANTI-SLIP FINISH

LAMINATE GLASS (TOP TOUGHENED)

NEOPRENE STRIP

STEEL FLAT

STEEL FLAT

SILICONE

CONTINUOUS KICK RAIL

GLASS TILES

BALL SOCKET CONNECTION (SEE DETAIL)

FINE THREAD VERTICAL ADJUSTMENT TURNBUCKLE

ARM CONNECTION TO RAMP DETAIL

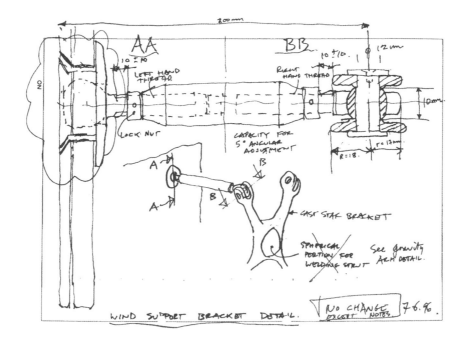

200 mm

AA

BB

NO

LEFT HAND THREAD

10 + 10

RIGHT HAND THREAD

10 + 10

12 mm

4

10 mm

LOCK NUT

CAPACITY FOR 5° ANGULAR ADJUSTMENT

R = 18.

r = 17 mm

A

A

B

B

CAST STAR BRACKET

SPHERICAL PORTION FOR WELDING STRUT

See gravity ARM DETAIL.

WIND SUPPORT BRACKET DETAIL.

NO CHANGE EXCEPT NOTES   7·6·96.

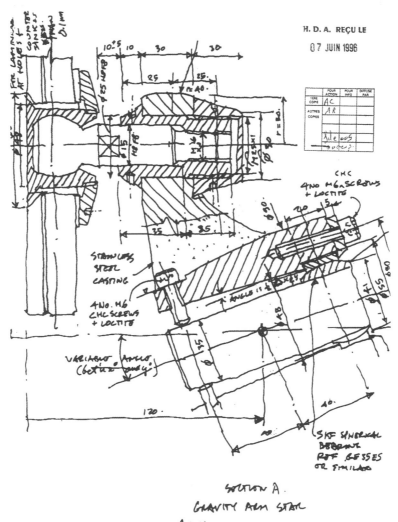

	POUR ACTION	POUR INFO	DIFFUSE PAR
1ERE COPIE	AC		
AUTRES COPIES	AR		
	File 005		
	Sucher?		

STAINLESS STEEL CASTING

4No. M6 CHC SCREWS + LOCTITE

CHC 4No M6n SCREWS + LOCTITE

VARIABLE ANGLE (between 0 and 4°)

ANGLE IS 4°

SKF SPHERICAL BEARING REF GE55ES OR SIMILAR

FIRE LAMINUM AT HOLES?

SOLUTION A.
GRAVITY ARM STAR
A∠H. 7.6.96 H.D.

75

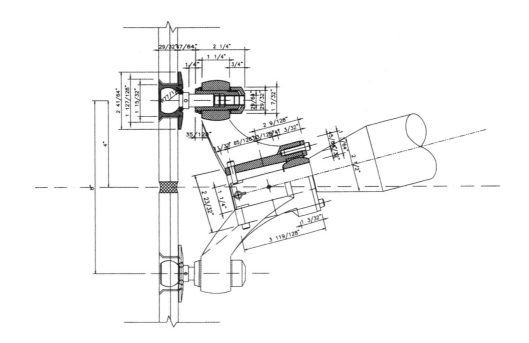

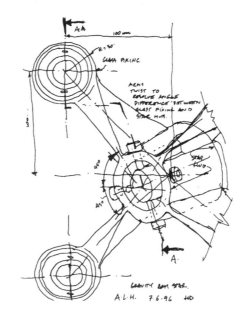

GRAVITY ARM STAR.
A.L.H. 7.6.96 HD

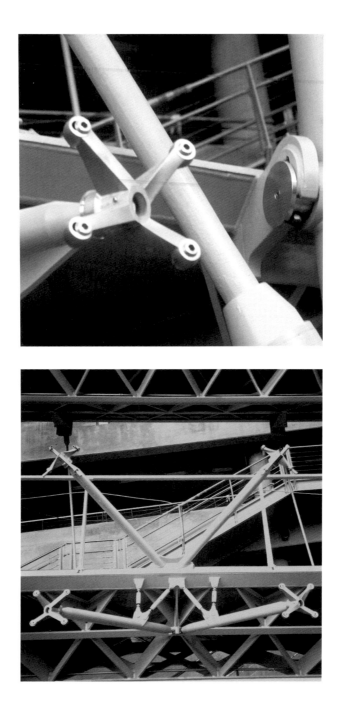

Structural Diagrams

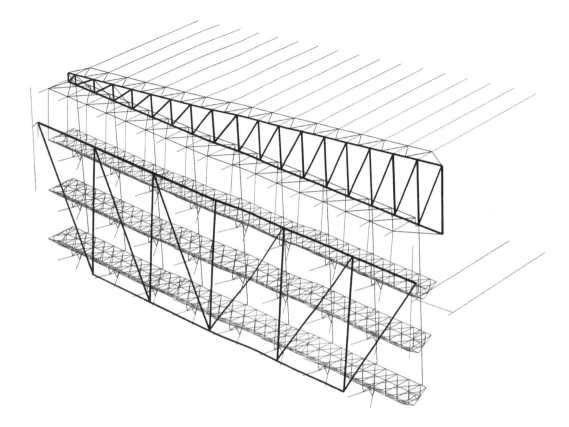

Primary Trusses

The vertical loads on the structure are supported by two primary trusses, which span 100ft between the base building structure, providing a column-free zone at ground level. The Inclined Facade Truss (IFT) is set close to the glazing plane and vertically supports one side of the ramps; the other side is hung off the high-level Roof Transfer Truss (RTT), which also supports the hub roof. Vertical glazing is hung directly off the ramps and skylight structure by gravity support arms.

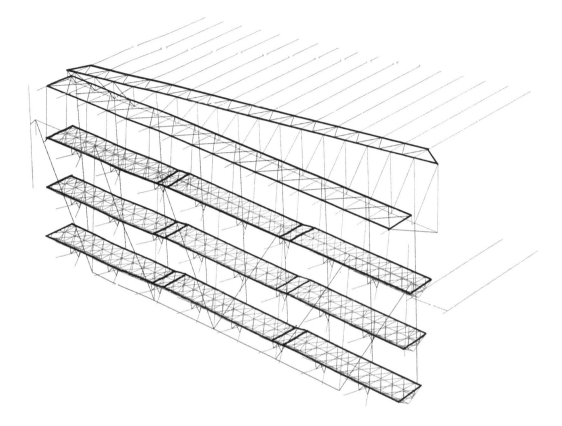

Primary Horizontal Bracing Planes

Wind loads on the vertical glazing are transferred back to the base building frame by five horizontal bracing planes. The lower three of these are formed by the ramps, which act as horizontal beams. Above them the skylight roof is braced to form a wind truss and the hub roof acts as a stiff diaphragm at the top. Seismic loads perpendicular to the glazing plane are carried in a similar manner. Seismic loads in this direction are not critical as wind load dominates.

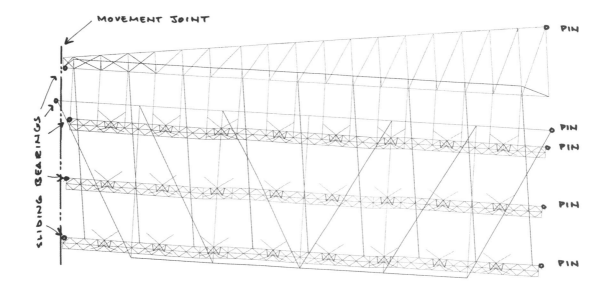

MOVEMENT JOINT

PIN

PIN
PIN

PIN

PIN

SLIDING BEARINGS

Connections to Base Building Frame

Seismic loads parallel to the glazing plane are transferred back to the base building by the ramps and primary trusses. A movement joint was introduced at the eastern interface with the base building structure at Grid Line 7. This isolates the wall from differential movements between the two wings of the base building, and allows expansion and contraction of the glass wall under thermal loads. Sliding bearings were incorporated into all of the primary connections to the base building structure at Grid Line 7.

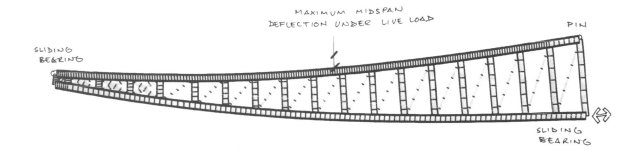

MAXIMUM MIDSPAN
DEFLECTION UNDER LIVE LOAD

PIN

SLIDING
BEARING

SLIDING
BEARING

Roof Transfer Truss

The Roof Transfer Truss (RTT) spans 100ft between the base building structure, and has to be very stiff vertically to reduce the movements generated in the glazing plane by live-loading on the ramps. W14x235 Jumbo sections were adopted as chords to limit the midspan deflection under live loading to 3in (span/1000).

The shape of the truss – generated by the geometry of the skylight and hub rooflines – suggests that it could act as a propped cantilever, fixed at its western end. This action, however, would generate significant diaphragm forces in the base building slabs, adding

complexity and cost to the structure overall. In order to prevent transfer of these forces, a sliding bearing was introduced at the connection of the bottom chord to the base building frame at Grid Line 4. The top chord is connected with a $5\frac{1}{2}$in steel pin connection, while the truss connection at the eastern end sits on a sliding bearing.

For scheduling reasons the RTT was incorporated into the base building steelwork package along with the hub roof beams. The RTT was fabricated in two pieces, bolted together on site, and lifted into place.

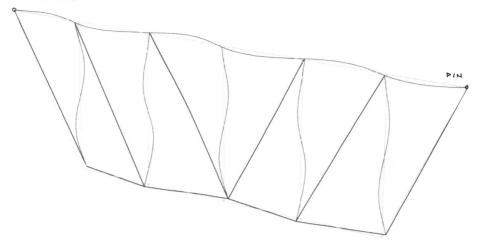

SLIDING BEARING

PIN

Inclined Facade Truss

The Inclined Facade Truss (IFT) is set between the ramps and the glass plane, so it was desirable to minimize the visual bulk of its components. As with the RTT, a high degree of stiffness was sought to limit the effects of ramp live-loading on the vertical glazing. This led to the development of a deep truss with a span-to-depth ratio of around 3.5:1, limiting deflection at the centre of the truss under ramp live-load to 3in (span/2000).

The truss form is divided into tension components (bottom chord and truss diagonals) and compression components (top chord and truss diagonals). Tension elements are solid steel rods of 2in and 3in diameter, and compression elements are $7\,^5/_8$ in pipe sections.

The size of the compression elements in such a deep truss is dictated by their buckling behaviour. The truss has negligible stiffness out of plane and so is restrained by the three ramps perpendicular to the glazing plane. These connections, however, create a problem – because the top and bottom ramps are tied in to the chords of the IFT, they attract high axial forces from the overall truss action of the structure. A sliding bearing was incorporated into the pin connection between the ramp and the IFT verticals to allow free movement along the axis of the ramps, to release the forces. The truss verticals are fully tied in at their midpoint to Ramp 2. This is possible because the ramp lies along the neutral axis of the IFT.

The buckling behaviour of the system was analysed using non-linear analysis techniques to verify the adequacy of the restraint provided to IFT compression elements.

The truss was fabricated in pieces and assembled on site at ground level. Site connections in compression elements are welded full-strength splices. Tension elements are typically pin-ended with a custom-machined steel end clevis. The bottom chord is made up of threaded rods, with a tapped connection to solid steel nodes at the base of the truss verticals. The curved end nodes are cast steel.

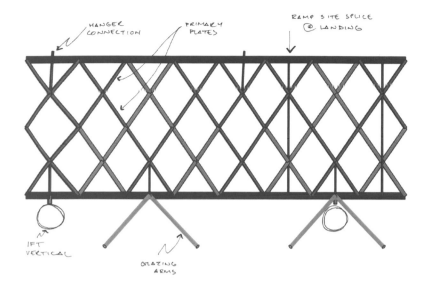

HANGER
CONNECTION

PRIMARY
PLATES

RAMP SITE SPLICE
@ LANDING

IFT
VERTICAL

GLAZING
ARMS

Ramp Elements

The form of the ramps was significantly influenced by visual considerations, with the structure conceived as a series of intersecting, triangulated plates. The diamond layout of the plates on plan acts as a natural bracing system with edge and bottom chords tying the plates together to form a three-dimensional truss capable of spanning 100ft horizontally.

The ramps are vertically supported at closer intervals, providing a redundancy in the system – ramps were analysed under an extreme loadcase where support from a tie was removed.

The ramps support the vertical glazing with gravity arms, hung from the bottom of the truss. The overturning generated by the glazing load is balanced out by the dead weight of the ramp, ensuring that the hanger ties do not go into compression.

The ramp plates are split into $\frac{5}{8}$in triangular primary plates and 3in x $\frac{5}{8}$in secondary struts. The primaries are arranged on an asymmetrical grid around major connection points to the glazing arms and IFT.

RTT hangers on the inner side of the ramps are set out on an opposing inclined grid to the ramps. This means that hanger connections are different for each of the three ramps. Ramp plates were locally strengthened to accommodate the varying conditions. Each ramp was fabricated in three sections, which were site-welded together at landings.

The ramp structure is regularly supported along its length, providing high vertical stiffness. This gives the ramps a relatively high natural frequency (around 10Hz), making them less prone to dynamic excitation by pedestrians. The RTT and IFT, which support the ramps, have a lower natural frequency but the overall weight they support limits dynamic accelerations to acceptable levels.

The ramp floor glazing is made up of two panes of $\frac{5}{16}$in tempered glass. This build up was developed and tested by the contractor for robustness using a test developed from Euro Code 1123, in which a 10lb ball is dropped from varying heights until failure occurs. The floor panels withstood impacts from up to 12ft before cracking of the lower pane occurred.

eif85 TOTAL RAMP MODEL
30522
7/13/97 from EIF84
p48 end of IFT as per Eif
dwgs
File: eif85.gwb

Part is excluded by volume

Scale: 1:134.5

Elem. Trans., Uy: 8.000 in/pic

941.0E-3 in
806.6E-3 in
672.2E-3 in
537.7E-3 in
403.3E-3 in
268.9E-3 in
134.4E-3 in
.0 in

Case: "WIND LOAD (30psf)"

Internal Arrangement

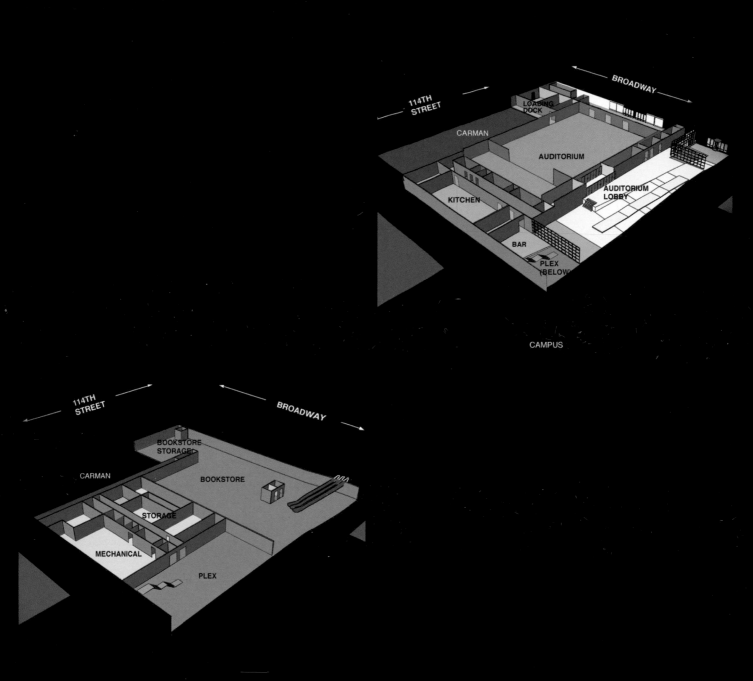

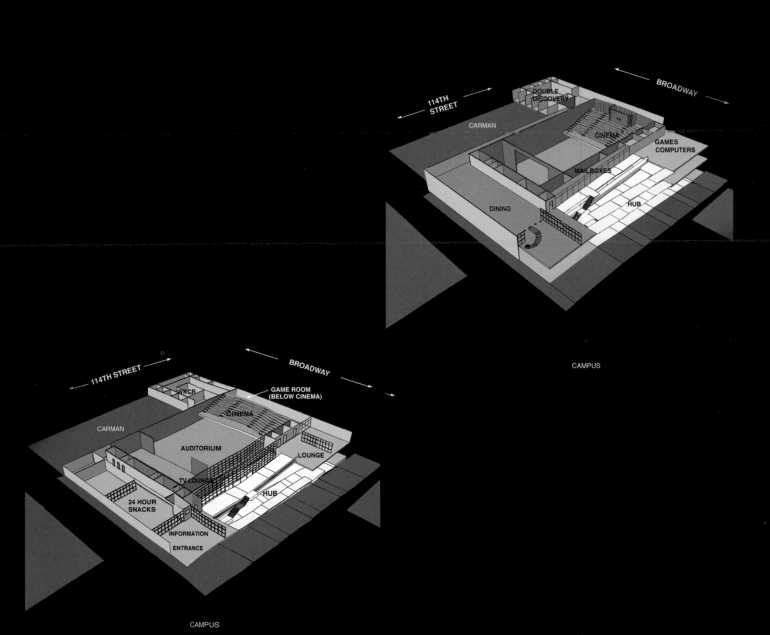

BROADWAY

114TH
STREET

DOUBLE
DISCOVERY

CARMAN

CINEMA

GAMES
COMPUTERS

MAILBOXES

DINING

HUB

CAMPUS

BROADWAY

114TH STREET

WKCR

GAME ROOM
(BELOW CINEMA)

CINEMA

CARMAN

AUDITORIUM

LOUNGE

TV LOUNGE

24 HOUR
SNACKS

HUB

INFORMATION

ENTRANCE

CAMPUS

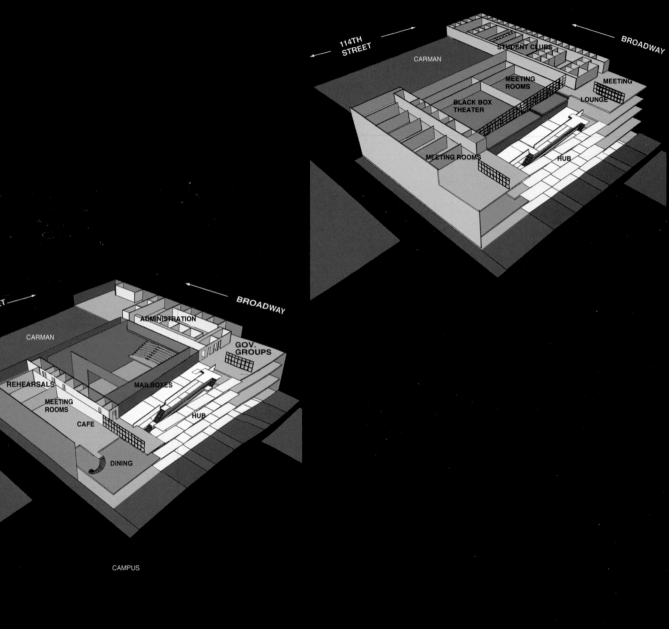

114TH STREET

BROADWAY

CARMAN

STUDENT CLUBS

MEETING ROOMS

BLACK BOX THEATER

MEETING

LOUNGE

MEETING ROOMS

HUB

114TH STREET

BROADWAY

CARMAN

ADMINISTRATION

GOV. GROUPS

REHEARSALS

MAILBOXES

MEETING ROOMS

CAFE

HUB

DINING

CAMPUS

Opening Night